C000057707

Somerset
Bath to the Quantocks

Compiled by
Dennis and Jan Kelsall

Text: Dennis and Jan Kelsall
Photography: Dennis and Jan Kelsall
Editorial: Ark Creative (UK) Ltd
Design: Ark Creative (UK) Ltd

© Crimson Publishing, a division of
Crimson Business Ltd

This product includes mapping data licensed from Ordnance Survey® with the permission of the Controller of Her Majesty's Stationery Office.
© Crown Copyright 2010. All rights reserved. Licence number 150002047. Ordnance Survey, the OS symbol and Pathfinder are registered trademarks and Explorer, Landranger and Outdoor Leisure are trademarks of the Ordnance Survey, the national mapping agency of Great Britain.

ISBN 978-1-85458-640-7

While every care has been taken to ensure the accuracy of the route directions, the publishers cannot accept responsibility for errors or omissions, or for changes in details given. The countryside is not static: hedges and fences can be removed, field boundaries can alter, footpaths can be rerouted and changes in ownership can result in the closure or diversion of some concessionary paths. Also, paths that are easy and pleasant for walking in fine conditions may become slippery, muddy and difficult in wet weather, while stepping-stones across rivers and streams may become impassable.

If you find an inaccuracy in either the text or maps, please write to Crimson Publishing at the address below.

First published 2002 by
Jarrold Publishing

This edition first published in Great Britain 2010 by Crimson Publishing, a division of:
Crimson Business Ltd
Westminster House, Kew Road
Richmond, Surrey, TW9 2ND
www.totalwalking.co.uk

Printed in Singapore. 3/10

A catalogue record for this book is available from the British library.

Front cover: Looking out from Bathford Hill
Previous page: Velvet Bottom

Contents

SCALE 1:384 615 or 1 INCH to about 6 MILES *1CM to 3.8KM*

0   2   4   6   8   10 KILOMETRES   15

0   2   4   6 MILES 8   10

KEYMAP HEIGHTS SHOWN IN METRES

Introduction

The routes and information in this book have been devised specifically with families and children in mind. All the walks include points of interest as well as a question to provide an objective.

If you, or your children, have not walked before, choose from the shorter walks for your first outings. The purpose is not simply to get from A to B but to enjoy an exploration, which may be just a steady stroll in the countryside.

The walks are graded by length and difficulty, but few landscapes are truly flat, so even shorter walks may involve some ascent. Details are given under Route Features in the first information box for each route. But the precise nature of the ground underfoot will depend on recent weather conditions. If you do set out on a walk and discover the going is harder than you expected, or the weather has deteriorated, do not be afraid to turn back. The route will always be there another day, when you are fitter or the children are more experienced or the weather is better.

Bear in mind that the countryside also changes. Landmarks may disappear, gates may become stiles, and rights of way may be altered. However, with the aid of this book and its maps you should be able to enjoy interesting family walks in the countryside.

Somerset – Bath to the Quantocks

From the breezy heights of Ham Hill to the vast levels and moors that lie barely above the sea, Somerset's landscapes are as varied and engagingly beautiful as any in the country, marking a division between the gentle, rolling countryside that epitomises England and something hinting of a more rugged and independent nature. Though sandwiched between the two, it has much that is uniquely its own, both expressed in its contours that have been fashioned and clothed by nature and the changes wrought by man since his first settlement. This selection of walks explores a part of that land, from Bath to the Quantocks, seeking out its different moods and introducing fascinating places that reflect its history and loveliness.

In following them, you will discover some of the best places to enjoy Somerset's natural scenery and wildlife habitats.

Monkton Farleigh

Somerset's uplands

In the east lies a band of oolitic limestone, part of the great swathe that sweeps across England from the Humber to Lyme Bay. Here, as elsewhere, it is valued as a building stone, and its subtle changes and textures are mirrored in the differing characters of the towns and villages that dot its undulating valleys and hilltops. In contrast is the landscape of the Mendip Hills, one of two Areas of Outstanding National Beauty (AONBs) in the county. Also of limestone, but of the carboniferous type, its complexion is hard, grey and bare, fractured by deep gorges and dry valleys that are honeycombed with spectacular caves such as those at Cheddar and Wookey. To the west lie the Quantock Hills, the country's first AONB. Founded on sandstones and shales, they are clad in a wonderful mantle of oaken woodland and heath. Their secluded combes and airy hilltops were a source of inspiration to the Romantic poets Coleridge and Wordsworth and, still relatively untouched, they are little short of a walkers' paradise.

The levels and coast

Yet another landscape type is found in the huge expanse of flatness that runs north from the Quantocks. Once a great fenland, the coastal levels and lower-lying peat moors that spread inland behind them have been reclaimed for farming over the centuries by the construction of a vast network of drainage ditches, called rhynes. Now a wetland site of considerable importance, it sustains a rich variety of animal and plant life. Somerset's coast is also worth exploring. Although lacking dramatic cliffs, it supports several important habitats and, with an outlook to the Welsh coast, almost any vantage guarantees a fine view on a clear day.

Perhaps surprisingly, the coast holds the record for the second-greatest tidal range in the world, varying by as much as 47ft (14m) between high and low water.

An ancient land

Relics of our prehistoric ancestors speckle the landscape, particularly on isolated hilltops and throughout the Mendips and the Quantocks. Several burial mounds from the Stone and Bronze Ages and hillforts and settlements from the Iron Age are featured, each spectacular in its own way. Around Priddy, you will almost lose count of the burial monuments passed. Dowsborough Hillfort commands one of the finest strategic views in the county. We follow in the footsteps of the Romans, from the Mendip lead mines to the top of Ham Hill, where they conquered one of Europe's largest hillforts and began stone quarries that are still worked today.

After the Romans

Somerset lay at the heart of Anglo-Saxon Wessex, and it was at Athelney, on the marshes below Stoke St Gregory, that Alfred the Great is held to have burnt the cakes. Alfred was a Christian king, and many of the village churches can trace some link to the Saxon era. King Ine founded Muchelney's first abbey in the 8th century and the later location of a Cluniac priory at Montacute might have been influenced by its proximity to the sacred Saxon site of St Michael's Hill.

A narrowboat on the Somerset Coal Canal

Man's legacy

The church is often the oldest building in a community and many aspects of the place's history can be gleaned from its stones and monuments, which offer a tapestry of changing architectural style. Those visited have some wonderful examples of English craftsmanship, with carvings in both wood and stone, paintings and stained glass. The walks pass other buildings too, allowing you to contrast the ruins of a medieval castle with those of a much earlier Norman fortification. Architecture from later periods is also represented, such as the Priest's House at Muchelney, and a splendid Elizabethan mansion at Montacute. At Iford there is an opportunity to visit a wonderful garden laid out at the beginning of the 20th century by the architect Harold Peto.

Not to be overlooked is Somerset's commercial past. Bristol was once a major port but centuries before that, the Romans exported lead from the Mendips across their empire. During the medieval period, a whole host of industries thrived. Many were based on the wool and cloth, but tanning and leather, paper, quarrying and coal and metal ore mining were among those also important in creating wealth. At Wookey you will find a working paper mill, and hidden in a valley outside Mells are the remains of a once-busy iron foundry. Walk from Stoke St Gregory and you can learn about one of Somerset's oldest trades, willow weaving, still carried out using traditional materials and methods. The routes also touch on the transport revolution that had a large part to play in boosting Somerset's economy during the industrialisation of Britain. The Kennet and Avon Canal was built to link Bristol and London and its two aqueducts, at Avoncliff and by Monkton Combe, carrying it above the Avon gorge, were spectacular achievements of their time. The railways followed about 100 years later, criss-crossing the county with their maze of tracks. Much of the network was abandoned during the middle of the 20th century, a victim to the convenience of road transport. But the courses of some are now designated footpaths, and like that across the marshes at Langport, support a rich variety of plants.

The whole area is well covered by an extensive web of quiet tracks and paths, and several long-distance trails have been created, such as the riverside Parrett Trail, and the Greenway, which links the villages and hamlets around the foot of the Quantocks. With so much diversity and a wealth of interesting places, it can be difficult to decide just where to go. But this collection guides you to some of the most rewarding places, whetting your appetite to discover more of this county.

1 *Cadbury Camp*

START Tickenham

DISTANCE 2¾ miles (4.4km)

APPROXIMATE TIME 1½ hours

PARKING Lay-by opposite Tickenham church

ROUTE FEATURES Moderate climb, field paths and lane

Dotted about the Somerset moors like islands, which indeed many of them once were, are numerous hills. Dry havens offering superb vantages over the surrounding countryside, they attracted the earliest inhabitants of the area, and many bear traces of ancient settlement. Few, however, are as impressive as Cadbury Camp, the object of this interesting walk, which climbs a high ridge overlooking Nailsea.

The church at Tickenham

With the church on your right, follow Church Lane onto the Causeway, leaving just after the bend over a stile beside a gate on the right onto Tickenham Moor. Walk away beside the boundary, which later curves right to a gate. Continue beside a ditch to a humped bridge and another gate. Bear left beyond to join and follow the field edge. Right of the corner, a bridge and stile lead to a small enclosure. Follow a fence to a stile beneath a horse chestnut tree opposite; from here an enclosed path rises to Clevedon Road **A**.

PUBLIC TRANSPORT Bus service from Bristol and Clevedon along the B3130 (alternative start)

REFRESHMENTS The Star Inn, to the east along the B3130

ORDNANCE SURVEY MAPS Explorer 154 (Bristol West & Portishead), Landranger 172 (Bristol & Bath)

Cross and go left to a way-marked path leaving through a gate between two houses 50 yds along. Through a kissing-gate at the top take the path branching left, which undulates within the fringe of Baye's Wood. Remain with the main trail, which eventually curves right and ascends more steeply to a stile. Continue upward, the trees thinning to grazing, and leave over a stile beside a gate at the top left corner **B**.

> **?** *How was the way into Cadbury Camp defended?*

Turn right onto a broad track, Cadbury Camp Lane West, which climbs over the hill. On a clear day, there are fine views both across the Bristol Channel and inland over the levels, and just ahead, to the right, are the western ramparts of Cadbury hillfort. Beyond the

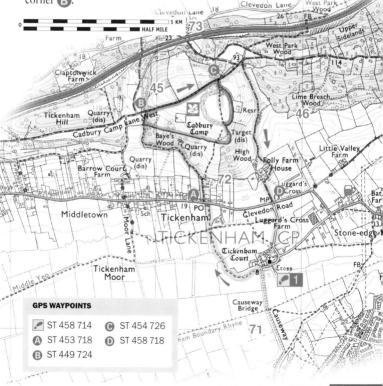

GPS WAYPOINTS

🚩 ST 458 714	**C** ST 454 726
A ST 453 718	**D** ST 458 718
B ST 449 724	

Although dated as a late **Iron Age camp**, the find of a bronze spearhead suggests an even earlier occupation. Cadbury's earthen banks and complex entrance are an impressive sight, but imagine them much higher and crowned by a stake fence, a formidable obstacle to any would-be attacker already wearied by climbing the hill. However, such defences were little deterrent to the Romans, and although nothing suggests that they took the place by force, the discovery of an altar stone to the god Mars and a double-ditched, square enclosure, probably a Roman marching-camp, indicate they too valued its strategic position.

summit, the track descends into trees, shortly passing a stile into the camp **C**.

Return to the track and carry on downhill. Reaching houses, the way becomes metalled. Turn beside the first house on the right to a gate and descend along a grass track marked as a bridleway. Walking above a golf course, wind around Folly Farm to meet a tarmac drive. Cross and continue down to the main road **D**. Washing Pound Lane opposite leads you back to the church. ●

The dedication to St Quiricus and St Julietta, two Roman martyrs, suggests an early foundation to the **church**, and traces of Saxon construction can be found in its stonework. More evidence of early settlement lies just to the west, where a low ring work was the site of a 12th-century castle. It was built during the first English civil war, when Stephen and Matilda fought for the throne after the death of Henry I. Tickenham Court, now a farm, is centred on a great hall, which was built in the 14th century and extended some 200 years later.

The view towards Brean Down from Cadbury Camp

Brean Down

A stiff climb at the beginning is quickly rewarded by magnificent views in every direction. The walk continues with an easy, undulating stroll, which eventually drops to an impressive fort at the tip of the promontory. Recently restored, it provides a fascinating glimpse to a time when Britain was being fortified against an expected invasion by Napoleon III.

START Brean Bird Garden
DISTANCE 3 miles (4.8km)
APPROXIMATE TIME 1½ hours
PARKING Car park at start
ROUTE FEATURES Steep climb at start of walk, *unguarded cliff edges*

2

The southern flank of Brean Down, jutting out into the Bristol Channel, runs for over a mile in an unbroken line of rounded cliffs, almost 200ft (61m) high. The way up is by a long stepped path, which you will find behind the Bird Garden. Pause for a well-earned rest at the top, beside the ruins of a wartime observation point **A**.

The fort on Brean Down was blown up in 1900, but not by any invading army, what happened?

All the hard work is now over and the route to the first summit lies left, along a gently climbing grassy path. At just under 260ft (79m)

Although bounded by cliffs and steep slopes, the top of **Brean Down** is relatively level and was large enough to support a prehistoric settlement. Cleared of its trees, the land was suitable for both grazing and agriculture, and the cliffs and surrounding sea provided a natural defence against the opportunist raids of neighbouring clans. The low earthworks around the summit triangulation pillar trace boundaries between ancient fields.

PUBLIC TRANSPORT Bus service from Weston-super-Mare
REFRESHMENTS Café at Bird Garden
PUBLIC TOILETS Near car park
PLAY AREA In Jubilee Park, by the car park
ORDNANCE SURVEY MAPS Explorer 153 (Weston-super-Mare & Bleadon Hill), Landranger 182 (Weston-super-Mare)

above the sea, the top provides stunning views along the Channel as well as inland across the levels. It is easy to imagine this as the island it once was, before the marshes were finally drained to provide valuable pasture on which cattle could be grazed.

Ahead, the way falls before rising again to the second summit, which, at an altitude of almost 320ft (97m), is the highest point of the ridge. As you continue, there is a wonderful view across the Channel, straight to Steep Holm, which lies about 3½ miles out to sea. The other island farther away to the right is Flat Holm and has a lighthouse on its rocky point. The path follows the length of the ridge down, ultimately dropping right to

the fort at its western end **B**.

Rather than climb back to the top of the ridge, you can return along the former military road, a track contouring the less-steep northern flank of the outcrop.

Howe Roc
Brean D
(dis

> The **fort** was one of many built along the country's coasts during the 1870s to resist an expected invasion by the French. Although rumours abounded that secret agents, and even Napoleon himself, landed by night at secluded coves along the south coast, the assault never came. The defences were re-armed during the two World Wars and the remnants of military occupation from both centuries now lie side by side.

The view across the bay to Weston-super-Mare

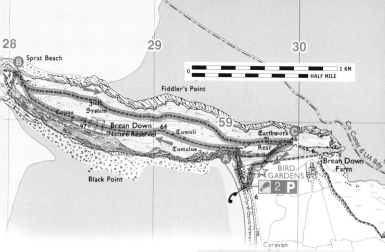

Towards the far end, just after the track crests, look over to the right to see an earthwork. It is thought to be a pillow mound, heaped up during the medieval period to establish a rabbit warren. Shortly beyond there, the track turns

GPS WAYPOINTS

  📍 ST 296 585   **B** ST 280 583

  A ST 295 588   **C** ST 299 588

around the eastern end of the down **C** and drops back to the Bird Garden.   ●

Brean Down overlooking miles of sandy beach

3 Around Burrington Combe

START	Foot of Burrington Combe
DISTANCE	3½ miles (5.6km)
APPROXIMATE TIME	2 hours
PARKING	Roadside car park at start
ROUTE FEATURES	Moderate climb, woodland paths

Overlooked by Black Down, the highest point of the Mendip Hills, Burrington Combe is a dark and narrow chasm that is now a dry valley. Although the road through is busy and offers little pleasure to the walker, this route around its surrounding hills offers glimpses into the gorge's wooded depths and delightful views across the countryside.

🖊 From the car park, walk down past the Burrington Inn and garden centre, and then turn right into a lane, Ham Link. Follow it up to a junction by a triangular green and bear right. Continue climbing to the top of the hill and then go right onto a marked bridleway Ⓐ.

Climb through woodland on a gradually rising path, which ultimately winds up meeting a broad track. Walk left and continue the ascent, now on more open heath. Follow the main path up a last rise, which eases towards the top. There is then a fine view back across the countryside to the coast.

Over the crest, the path now falls gently past a track from the left. Carry on ahead, the way subsequently joined by a footpath from the right. It leads across the nature reserve to Long Rock, the high point on the

Although smaller and, perhaps, less-obviously dramatic than its near neighbour, Cheddar Gorge, **Burrington Combe** was formed by a similar process. Its cliff-like sides, however, are almost obscured by trees, which manage to find a foothold in the crevices of the rock.

REFRESHMENTS Café and pub at foot of Burrington Combe
PUBLIC TOILETS Adjacent to car park at start of walk
ORDNANCE SURVEY MAPS Explorer 141 (Cheddar Gorge & Mendip Hills West), Landranger 182 (Weston-super-Mare)

common, and the splendid views from there make it a worthy detour. However, the onward route lies ahead, soon dropping through a belt of trees to emerge onto the road at the top of the combe **B**.

A refuge during a storm inspired the famous hymn

Turn left and walk up the road for about 200 yds to a bridleway on the right. A gently rising track leads to an open heath beneath Beacon Batch. At a crossing **C**, turn right and then fork right. At a waymark, just

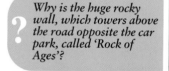
Why is the huge rocky wall, which towers above the road opposite the car park, called 'Rock of Ages'?

GPS WAYPOINTS

✒ ST 476 587	**C** ST 490 577
A ST 481 590	**D** ST 474 586
B ST 489 581	

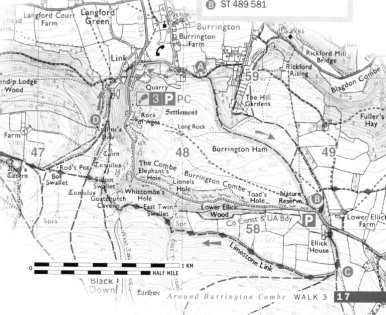

The view north from the top of Burrington Ham

farther on, the route divides to run either as a footpath through the perimeter of the trees or a wider bridlepath at the edge of the moor.

The way now undulates easily along the fringe of open heath and occasionally offers fine views across Burrington Combe through breaks in the trees. Farther on, the route dips to cross the head of a wooded gully, East Twin Swallet, emerging only to dip again across a second gully shortly after.

Keep going, ignoring crossing paths and eventually arriving at a prominent waymarked crossing. Turn right and follow it down, before long reaching a stone track opposite a wooden cabin **D**.

In spring and early summer, the limestone commons support a rich variety of **flowers** such as wild thyme, marjoram and rock rose, which in turn encourage numerous **insects**. Keep your eyes open for butterflies such as the common blue and meadow brown, and the strikingly patterned burnet moth. There are lots of grasshoppers here too. Walk quietly through the woods and you just might catch a glimpse of a roe deer.

Go right again, the track descending past occasional cottages and later becoming metalled. Now take a path off to the right, signed 'RUPP' (road used as public footpath). After a short drop, it ends beside a cottage. Walk out to the road, where the Burrington Inn then lies just to the right. ●

● Dramatic gorge ● views ● spectacular caves ● paper mill

Wookey and Ebbor Gorge

START Wookey
DISTANCE 2¼ miles (3.6km)
APPROXIMATE TIME 1 hour
PARKING Roadside parking in village (car park for visitors to Wookey Hole only)
ROUTE FEATURES Steep climb; *rocks slippery when wet;* country lanes without footpaths

4

Although perhaps best known for its splendid caves, which burrow into the limestone of the Mendip Hills behind the village, Wookey has some equally magnificent scenery above the ground. This walk goes in search of that, in Ebbor Gorge. It lies just to the north-west, a deep, narrow, wooded ravine, through which an impressive path climbs to the hillside above.

✎ Walk out of the village past Wookey Hole, bearing right at a junction towards Easton and Cheddar. Some 250 yds along, immediately after the last cottage on the right, turn beside it through a gate, signed 'Priddy and West Mendip Way' Ⓐ.

Bear left along the foot of a wooded hillside field and soon climb over a stile into a wood at the bottom of Ebbor Gorge. Ignore a stepped path off to the right but, at a fork just beyond it, go right, signed 'Gorge'.

Shortly, as the valley narrows, the path steepens and the way

A footpath rising to the narrow gorge

PUBLIC TRANSPORT Bus service from Wells
REFRESHMENTS Pubs in village, café at Wookey Hole Visitor Centre
PUBLIC TOILETS At Wookey Hole Visitor Centre
ORDNANCE SURVEY MAPS Explorer 141 (Cheddar Gorge & Mendip Hills West), Landranger 182 (Weston-super-Mare)

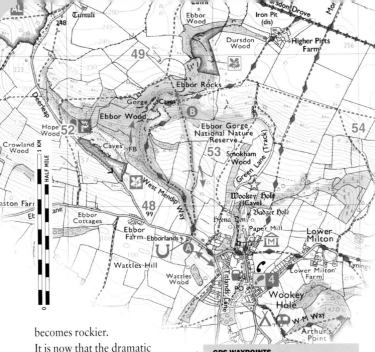

becomes rockier.

It is now that the dramatic nature of the gorge asserts itself, with high cliffs rising sheer on both sides. At one point it is just about possible to touch both sides at

GPS WAYPOINTS

✎ ST 532 475   Ⓑ ST 527 486

Ⓐ ST 528 478

once. Little legs may find the path a bit of a scramble, but there is nothing difficult. *However, do go carefully, particularly if it is wet, for the smooth limestone underfoot can be slippery.* Near the top of the climb is a rocky platform to the left above the path, from which

Ebbor Gorge is one of several deep and narrow ravines that cleave the steep, southern escarpment of the Mendip plateau. The river torrent that gouged it from the hard rock has long since disappeared, leaving dry the rocky river bed and steps, over which waterfalls once cascaded. Sheltered from the weather and largely untouched by man's activity, a lush woodland habitat has developed in which a rich variety of both plant and animal life thrives.

? *Where in Wookey will you find an elephant, a ghost and a witch's turkey?*

Wookey Hole is a series of chambers dissolved from the rock and containing countless fascinating formations. In places, the River Axe runs beneath your feet, its deceptively placid waters flowing at the rate of 11m gallons (50m litres) a day. Much of Wookey's spectacular cave system is still flooded by the river, but divers have penetrated some of the higher chambers. Their discoveries, together with archaeological finds, are displayed in the cave museum.

there is a spectacular view down the gorge.

Suddenly, the valley opens out and the climb eases, the route taking you, once again, into thick woodland. At a bend, go right, following a car park sign. Ascend a bank to a crossing of paths, where the car park is then signed right.

However, instead, now walk ahead on a fainter path, which drops through the trees to emerge over a stile at the top of an open field **B**.

As you descend the hillside beyond, there is a wonderful view across Wookey to Wells. Through a gap in the bottom hedge, carry on down the subsequent fields. Finally, at the foot of the hill, you meet your outward course. Return to the lane **A** and turn left for the short walk back to the village. ●

Children will enjoy visiting Wookey's **paper mill**, the oldest of its kind still working in the country and producing high-quality paper from cotton fibre by a process unchanged in centuries. Papermaking began here in 1610, exploiting both the power and purity of the River Axe.

Fields overlooking Wookey and Wells

5 *Kilve Pill and East Quantoxhead*

START Kilve Pill
DISTANCE 3 miles (4.8km)
APPROXIMATE TIME
1½ hours
PARKING Coastal car park
(Pay and Display)
ROUTE FEATURES Field
paths may be muddy
after rain; quiet lanes
without footpaths

Barely 5 miles wide but running for 14 miles in a gentle curve across Somerset, the Quantock Hills are everywhere full of charm and character. Here at their northern extremity, where they meet the Bristol Channel, the Quantocks present a rounded shoulder of soft, undulating hills to the sea, and this walk highlights just one more aspect of their individuality.

Go back along the lane by which you arrived at the car park. Beyond the ruined chantry and adjacent tea garden is Kilve church. There, turn in beneath the lychgate Ⓐ.

Leave the churchyard through a kissing-gate just past the porch and walk at the field edge out to a track. Follow it left past a junction and on over a stream. Continue across the fields to the corner of East Wood. Carry on below the edge of the trees, eventually leaving through a gate in the far corner of the field. Keep straight on along a track, which leads up to a junction in the hamlet of East Quantoxhead. Turn right and then left into a field, used as a car park and head across to visit the church Ⓑ.

The Church of **St Mary the Virgin** at Kilve Pill was founded around the 13th century and, like the nearby chantry, is said to have been used by smugglers, who landed cargoes on this lonely coast under cover of darkness. On one occasion, suspicious excise men apparently set fire to the chantry after being refused admission to search it for contraband.

PUBLIC TRANSPORT Bus service from Bridgwater to nearby Kilve village
REFRESHMENTS Tea garden and picnic area at Kilve Pill, tearoom at East Quantoxhead
PUBLIC TOILETS Adjacent to Kilve Pill car park
ORDNANCE SURVEY MAPS Explorer 140 (Quantock Hills & Bridgwater), Landranger 181 (Minehead & Brendon Hills)

At the heart of **East Quantoxhead** lies the **Court House**. A medieval building, it has been remodelled several times by the Luttrells, who have held the manor since the early 1400s. The adjacent church, also dedicated to St Mary the Virgin, was built in the 13th century and contains many interesting features. Look for the carvings on the pews and the unusual opening in the side of the porch, a 'coffin squint', which allowed the waiting priest to watch for the approach of a funeral.

Leaving the churchyard gate, bear right down to a field gate. Continue in the same direction across the subsequent field, to leave by another gate at the far corner. Turn right along the lane, but at a left-hand bend go ahead along an ascending, hedged

Where can you find a dove of peace and a unicorn at East Quantoxhead?

track. When you reach a junction at the crest of the hill **C** turn right onto a permissive path along the field edges to the coast.

Low cliffs of finely striated, soft shales fall below the coastal fields, and a path over a stile on the right takes you along their top. Undulating gently downwards, keep going along the perimeter

GPS WAYPOINTS

🖉 ST 144 443	**C** ST 129 431
A ST 147 439	**D** ST 136 441
B ST 136 436	

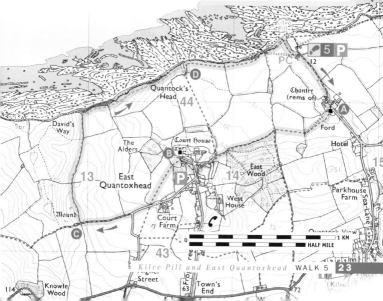

The path to the beach at Kilve Pill

rock. However, the route continues along the cliff path to Kilve Pill. There, you will find a grassy picnic area and you can again reach the beach. A path on the right then returns to the car park. ●

Inside the church at East Quantoxhead

of successive fields until you are forced inland beside a narrow inlet. Walk up past a ruined limekiln **D**, half-hidden by encroaching vegetation, and then double back around it, joining a track to return to the cliffs.

At this point, steps lead down to the shore, where a spring gushes from the cliffs – and you might discover a fossil in the crumbling

Will's Neck and the Triscombe Stone

START Triscombe

DISTANCE 3½ miles (5.6km)

APPROXIMATE TIME 2 hours

PARKING Lay-by up lane marked 'unsuitable for motor vehicles' above Blue Ball Inn

ROUTE FEATURES Woodland and heath paths, steep climb

6

Although lower than many hill areas, the Quantocks are defined by close-packed contours, denoting steep-flanking slopes. Obvious too are narrow valleys, splitting each side, which sometimes rise almost to meet at the middle. This ramble takes an oblique line to Will's Neck, the highest point on the range, before returning down one of its finest combes.

Continue up the lane a short distance beyond the parking area, looking for a discretely waymarked path on the right that doubles back above the lane. An easy walk through the trees then contours the hillside above the pub, eventually joining a lane **A**.

Immediately fork left onto a gently rising track, the Quantock Greenway. Keep right where it later

? *What are the huge trees that form an impressive avenue by the Triscombe Stone?*

forks, and follow it on through the woods until you ultimately drop to a junction **B**. To the left, a bridleway ascends the steep flank of Bagborough Hill. Keep climbing at a crossing track partway up. Eventually the trees thin, the gradient eases, and the track along the top of the ridge is not far ahead. Although there is still height to gain, the hard work is over, and it is now an enjoyable walk to the summit cairn of Will's Neck, which lies less than ½ mile to the left.

At the triangulation pillar **C**, where there is a superb view along

REFRESHMENTS Blue Ball Inn

ORDNANCE SURVEY MAPS Explorer 140 (Quantock Hills & Bridgwater), Landranger 181 (Minehead & Brendon Hills)

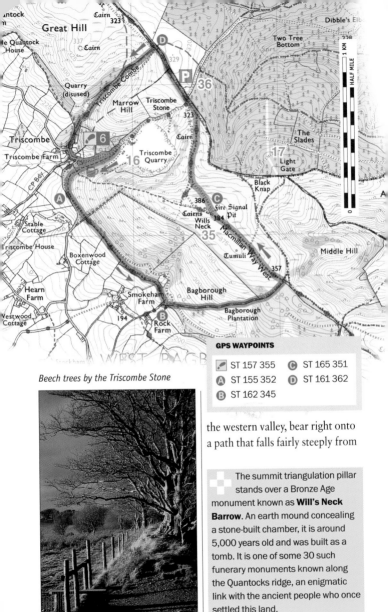

Beech trees by the Triscombe Stone

GPS WAYPOINTS

📏 ST 157 355   Ⓒ ST 165 351

Ⓐ ST 155 352   Ⓓ ST 161 362

Ⓑ ST 162 345

the western valley, bear right onto a path that falls fairly steeply from

The summit triangulation pillar stands over a Bronze Age monument known as **Will's Neck Barrow**. An earth mound concealing a stone-built chamber, it is around 5,000 years old and was built as a tomb. It is one of some 30 such funerary monuments known along the Quantocks ridge, an enigmatic link with the ancient people who once settled this land.

The ancient Triscombe Stone – the subject of strange tales

The low boulder by the junction is the **Triscombe Stone**, the name deriving from 'trist' – a meeting place. Its origins are lost in time, but some describe it as an ancient wishing stone. However, others warn of a more sinister purpose, saying that the Devil musters his spectral Yeth hounds and horsemen around it before embarking upon a frantic hunt across the moors. To see or even hear the hounds means certain death.

the ridge. Keep going where it eventually levels and then join a track to the left, which leads to a junction of tracks near a car park.

Continue ahead past the junction along the drove, which is lined by magnificent, wind-swept trees. A little way beyond a gate, at a dip, turn through a waymarked gate on the left **D** and walk away, dropping easily downhill along a grassy path into the deepening fold of Triscombe Combe. Lower down a more prominent track develops. Later, ignore a footpath branching through a gate on the right and keep going, shortly leaving the open hillside through a gate. Stay with the track past a farm and, when you reach a lane at the bottom, turn left to a junction opposite the Blue Ball Inn. Go left again and then keep ahead back to the parking area.

7 *The willow beds around Stoke St Gregory*

START Stoke St Gregory
DISTANCE 2½ miles (4km)
APPROXIMATE TIME 1 hour
PARKING Roadside
parking by church
ROUTE FEATURES
Moderate climb; field
paths; quiet lanes
without footpaths

An important industry of the communities fringing the Somerset moors was weaving, using willow rods cultivated in beds on the marshy ground. This short walk passes one of the places where the craft is still practised, and an exhibition gives a fascinating insight into the process from planting to finished basket, as well as illustrating the area's natural history.

From the church, walk to a junction opposite the Royal Oak and go right. Turn left into Church Close and then right up a short cul-de-sac. You will find a footpath between the houses at its end. Over a stile, follow the field's right-hand hedge to emerge onto a lane **A**.

Turn left, but at a thatched cottage opposite a road junction, leave over a stile on the right. Walk away, continuing at the edge of a second field and on over a couple of stiles into a larger field. Now bear left, pass through a gap in the hedge by a power-line post and maintain your direction to another gap, lying partway along the left-hand hedge. Cross to the far corner of the next field and walk out to a gravel track. Follow it left out to a lane **B**.

> Above the doorway of **St Gregory's Church** is a 15th-century statue of the saint carrying his emblems, a dove, book and pen. Elected pope in 590, he sent the missionary Augustine to England, and his influence on the ecclesiastical music of his day is remembered in the 'Gregorian' chants.

PUBLIC TRANSPORT Bus service from Taunton
REFRESHMENTS Royal Oak at Stoke St Gregory, tearoom at Willows and Wetlands Visitor Centre
PUBLIC TOILETS Willows and Wetlands Visitor Centre
ORDNANCE SURVEY MAPS Explorer 128 (Taunton & Blackdown Hills), Landranger 193 (Taunton & Lyme Regis)

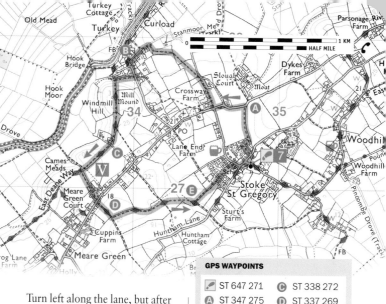

GPS WAYPOINTS

🖉 ST 647 271		ⓒ ST 338 272	
Ⓐ ST 347 275		ⓓ ST 337 269	
Ⓑ ST 339 278		ⓔ ST 343 269	

Turn left along the lane, but after 200 yds, cross a stile on the right. Follow the bottom field edge to another stile and then climb the hill by the left-hand hedge. Proceed through a gate at the top, passing a grass mound, the site of a post mill. Built entirely of wood, such mills were pivoted so that the whole building could be rotated to keep the sails facing the wind.

Carry on at the edge of the fields until you emerge beside the entrance of a small waste-water treatment plant ⓒ. Cross the drive and drop right to a stile. Continue beside the left hedge across successive fields until you reach a crossing track. There, go left out to a lane beside the Willows and Wetlands Visitor Centre.

A basketwork fish at the Willows and Wetlands Centre

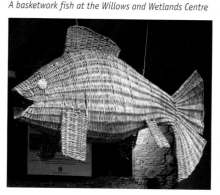

Just along the lane to the right, take a waymarked track on the left **D**, which leads into a field. Walk ahead but, as you pass into the subsequent field, turn left alongside the top hedge. Out across the levels north of east, the slender column rising on top of a

> Look for the stocks in St Gregory's churchyard. How many people can they accommodate?

wooded hill is a memorial to Sir Samuel Hood, who rose to admiral

A museum, video and weekday guided tours at the **Willows and Wetlands Visitor Centre** describe the different stages of willow production. Displays and exhibits also tell you something of how the area has evolved over the centuries and explain how man created the landscape we see today. They also illustrate some of the flowers and wildlife to be found in the different habitat

during the Napoleonic wars. Where the boundary later turns sharp left, keep ahead to find a stiled footbridge in the far-right corner of the field **E**. Cross and go right at the field edge. Ignore a bridge tucked in the corner and turn within the field to carry on beside its right-hand hedge. Leaving at the top, follow a contained path beside paddocks, continuing at the perimeter of a small field and between houses to emerge onto a street.

Keep going forward at the edge of a green and then beside a school to come out onto the main lane in Stoke St Gregory. Turn right and then left through the village to return to the Royal Oak.

A thatched roof under repair

Meare and the Abbot's Fish House

8

START Meare
DISTANCE 3¼ miles (5.2km)
APPROXIMATE TIME 1½ hours
PARKING Village car park in Muddy Lane
ROUTE FEATURES Field paths, lane

Once a vast marsh, the levels have a haunting atmosphere and rich history. This walk around Meare passes the site of prehistoric settlements and a medieval monastic grange.

From the car park, turn right through a gate along a broad, hedged path. At the end, go over a stile on the left and immediately turn right to walk the length of the field. Through a gate at the far side, keep going to a stiled footbridge in the middle of the bottom hedge. Continue beside the right hedge to a drainage ditch **A**. Cross a stile on the right and follow the watercourse at the bottom of successive narrow fields to Ashcott Road.

Over a stile opposite, keep by the ditch to another stile. Cross and turn right, walking up the field to a

gate and stile. Bear left to a stiled bridge partway along the left hedge. Continue the line to the top corner of the next field, emerging onto the bend of a narrow lane, Millbatch **B**.

In 1895, the sites of two **Iron Age settlements** were discovered to the north east of the present village. Low islands rising from the reed marsh, they are thought to have been seasonal trading posts. Interpretation of the pottery fragments, jewellery, animal bones and stone fragments found during excavation suggests the sites were used over the three centuries before the Romans arrived in Britain.

PUBLIC TRANSPORT Bus service from Glastonbury
REFRESHMENTS The Railway Inn, Ashcott Road
CHILDREN'S PLAY AREA By car park at start
ORDNANCE SURVEY MAPS Explorer 141 (Cheddar Gorge & Mendip Hills West), Landranger 182 (Weston-super-Mare)

A swan on Heath Rhyne

In which year was Meare School built?

when it finishes, joining a sparse hedge on the left that leads to the River Brue **D**.

Follow it right, passing at the foot of a succession of narrow enclosures until you reach a track by a graceful stone bridge. Cross and continue upstream to the next bridge. Re-cross and follow a narrow lane to its junction with the main lane **E**. From a gate on the right, a causey leads to the Abbot's Fish House.

> The extensive pools and lazy rivers of the marshes provided a ready source of fish, which was exploited by the abbey at Glastonbury. Fish was a regular part of the monk's diet, particularly during Lent when the consumption of meat was forbidden. Together with the manor house, the **fish house** provided comfortable accommodation for the monks overseeing the fishery and the orchards and vineyard that occupied the higher ground.

Ahead it shortly peters out past a house to end as a grass track. Over a stile beside the gate facing you, walk on by the left hedge. Carry on beyond its end straight across the field to Heath View Farm. Exit by the right-most gate into the farmyard and immediately turn right into another field. Head away beside the hedge, emerging onto the main lane in the village.

Go right but then take the second turning on the left, Meare Way **C**. Where that later bends left, keep ahead over a stile beside a gate into a farmyard. Over a stile in the left corner cross a small meadow to a stiled bridge and keep on by the right-hand hedge. Keep going

Continue across the field to a gate by Manor Farm. Walk in front of the farmhouse to another gate and immediately turn left along a walled path beside the church. Emerging on the main lane

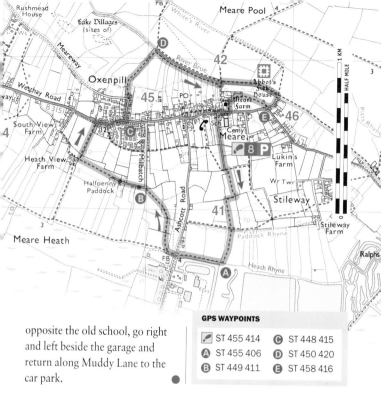

GPS WAYPOINTS

🥾 ST 455 414		**C** ST 448 415	
A ST 455 406		**D** ST 450 420	
B ST 449 411		**E** ST 458 416	

opposite the old school, go right and left beside the garage and return along Muddy Lane to the car park. ●

The Abbot's Fish House

9 Bathford Hill and Monkton Farleigh

START Bathford Hill

DISTANCE 4¼ miles (6.8km)

APPROXIMATE TIME 2 hours

PARKING Car park on minor lane above Bathford

ROUTE FEATURES Woodland and field paths; quiet lanes without pavements

East of Bath, the Avon squirms in a massive loop, contained within a deep, steep-sided valley below Bathford Hill. This walk winds through the lush woodland that fringes the top of the escarpment, where breaks in the trees frame grand views across the river. The return is by way of the village of Monkton Farleigh, an ancient monastic settlement.

From the rear of the car park, a few steps begin a meandering path that quickly turns from the lane into the woodland. At a fork, bear right and then keep ahead on the main path, passing entrances to some of the hill's abandoned mines. Eventually, the way emerges into a clearing, a long, open terrace below the upper cliff, which overlooks the Avon Valley and offers a magnificent view.

> **Bathford's** oolitic limestone has been exploited since Roman times, extracted by mining rather than quarrying to obtain the best stone. The stone workings were abandoned in the early 20th century, and lush woodland now covers the hillside. It is rich in both plant and animal life, and the dark recesses of the derelict mines are now home to bats.

Through a kissing-gate at the far side Ⓐ, the path returns to the wood. Ignore side paths and continue along a gently undulating path, which, after a mile descends to a road Ⓑ. About 100 yds along to the left, immediately after the gated entrance to a

PUBLIC TRANSPORT Bus service from Bath to Monkton Farleigh (alternative start)

REFRESHMENTS King's Arms at Monkton Farleigh

CHILDREN'S PLAY AREA Along lane above car park

ORDNANCE SURVEY MAPS Explorers 155 (Bristol & Bath) and 156 (Chippenham & Bradford-on-Avon), Landrangers 172 (Bristol & Bath) and 173 (Swindon & Devizes)

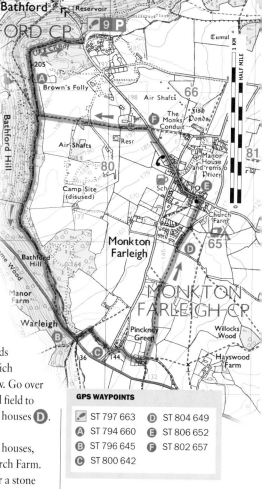

house, fork left and join a bridleway rising from a bridge beneath the road. At the top, it bends right, shortly leaving the trees to emerge at a junction beside Douch Farm Nursery **C**.

Cross to the minor lane opposite, taking the first right at a triangular green. Through a kissing-gate at the very end of the lane go left to a stile. Head out across successive fields towards Monkton Farleigh, which shortly comes into view. Go over a track and across a final field to meet a second track by houses **D**.

Keep ahead behind the houses, soon approaching Church Farm. Just before it, watch for a stone step leading up to a small wooden gate on the left. A contained path

> **?** What unusual structure is hidden in the left-hand bank of the lane after leaving Monkton Farleigh?

GPS WAYPOINTS

📍 ST 797 663	**D** ST 804 649
A ST 794 660	**E** ST 806 652
B ST 796 645	**F** ST 802 657
C ST 800 642	

leads around the edge of a paddock, continuing beside the church graveyard to come out in the village **E**.

Turn up the hill past St Peter's Church, which dates from the 13th century. It retains its original

Norman zigzag decoration above the door. Inside, is a fine, carved wooden pulpit from the Jacobean period.

Keep ahead at successive junctions to climb past the King's Arms. After 300 yds turn left onto a gated track **F**. Over a stile at the end, carry on across the field beyond. Go over a narrow lane and through a small copse to a tarmac track at the far side. Walk left and then fork right to continue between open fields to a gate into more woodland ahead. At the end of a short, walled path, turn right and walk beside the wall, soon reaching Brown's Folly.

Known locally as the 'Pepperpot', the tower was built in the 18th century by Mr Wade-Browne, who owned the manor house at nearby Monkton Farleigh. Its upper

A glimpse of the Avon Valley

The Cluniacs founded a priory in **Monkton Farleigh** in 1125, but after the Dissolution of the monasteries under Henry VIII in 1547 the estate passed to the Duke of Somerset. He built himself a manor house on the site, and all that remains today of the priory are ruins of the church's chancel wall. However, the strange-looking building in the field on the right beyond the King's Arms, known as the Monks' Conduit, covers a spring that supplied the monastery with water.

windows look out to the four points of the compass and a local tale suggests he built it so that he could spy on his wife whose fidelity he doubted.

Follow the woodland path ahead beyond the tower, ignoring side turnings and eventually joining your outward route for the short distance back to the car park. ●

During the Second World War, the deep underground quarries were used as a **munitions store**. Work began in 1937 in creating a railway siding at Box Bridge to the north. Until a rail tunnel to the heart of the mine and an underground sorting area were finished in 1941, ammunition was taken over the hill to the mine entrance by a camouflaged aerial ropeway. The store was only finally decommissioned during the 1960s.

The Kennet and Avon Canal and Monkton Combe

START Dundas Marina Visitor Centre

DISTANCE 3¾ miles (5.2km)

TIME 1½ hours

PARKING Car park at start (Pay and Display, locked at 21.00)

ROUTE FEATURES Canal towpaths, woodland and field paths, short climb

10

This is a nostalgic walk for those who remember The Titfield Thunderbolt, since Monkton Combe provided the Ealing comedy film with its village station. Sadly, the line and halt have now gone, but the street down which Titfield's inhabitants hurried to catch the morning train is still there. On summer Sunday afternoons, you can take a trip on the canal from the marina.

Start along a track from the rear of the car park, which follows the course of a former railway line below the marina. At the far end, the track rises to join the Kennet and Avon Canal towpath. The narrow entrance to the Somerset Coal Canal lies just to the left, but your onward route lies along the towpath to the right, over the Dundas Aqueduct Ⓐ.

At a bridge, ¾ mile farther on, leave the canal side to join the B3108 Ⓑ

The short section of canal now occupied by the marina is all that remains of the 10-mile **Somerset Coal Canal**. It operated between 1801 and 1898 and was built to service coal mines at Paulton and Radstock. The aqueduct is one of two that carry the **Kennet and Avon Canal** over the Avon and is named after Charles Dundas. He was chairman of the shareholders and raised £900,000 to finance the project. In its heyday, the canal carried almost 350,000 tons of cargo a year between London and Bristol.

PUBLIC TRANSPORT Bus service from Bath to Monkton Combe and Limpley Stoke and trains to Freshford near Limpley Stoke (alternative start)

REFRESHMENTS Café at marina, pubs in Limpley Stoke and Monkton Combe

CHILDREN'S PLAY AREA By route at Limpley Stoke

ORDNANCE SURVEY MAPS Explorer 155 (Bristol & Bath), Landranger 172 (Bristol & Bath)

and walk right across the River Avon and beneath a railway bridge to a junction. Go left into Limpley Stoke and, immediately after passing the Hop Pole Inn, turn right up Woods Hill. Bear right at a fork and then go right again at a junction, eventually reaching the main road at the top.

> **?** *How many arches support the viaduct carrying the A36 above Midford Brook?*

Cross to a path diagonally opposite **C**. After winding for some distance through unkempt woodland, the path drops steeply, emerging from the trees over a stile

above a field. Walk down, bearing left to a second stile, which takes you out onto the fork of a lane.

Take the lower lane on the left to Waterhouse, but approaching its gated drive, bear right. At the end in front of a gate to Mill Cottages turn right on a contained path swinging beside Midford Brook.

GPS WAYPOINTS

ST 782 621	**C** ST 779 609
A ST 784 625	**D** ST 774 618
B ST 783 612	**E** ST 775 622

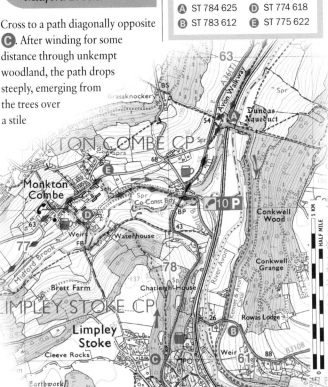

The building by the river, to the right of the mill stream bridge, was a **flax mill**, later adapted to manufacture cotton. After the market declined, it produced mattresses until the mill closed in the 1930s. The **railway** above was that of the Wiltshire, Somerset and Weymouth, and was built in the 1840s. It had already closed when the village was selected as the location for Titfield in the famous 1952 Ealing comedy. However, a section of track was reopened and the station refurbished for its starring role.

Climb a stone stile and go right over the stream. Carry on between rough enclosures to a second footbridge **D** spanning a mill stream.

The onward path climbs to join a lane, which crosses the courses of both the former railway and the coal canal. Continue up into Monkton Combe, passing a curious square building of stone on the right. It was built around 1776 as the village lock-up.

At the top by the Wheelwrights Arms, turn right through the village, passing some of its ancient buildings, which are now used by Monkton School. It was founded in 1868 by the Reverend Francis Pocock, vicar of St Michael's Church in the village, to educate the sons of missionaries.

Beyond the main school building **E**, turn into the school at a waymark. Walk down past the sports hall to a tarmac path, which continues through trees to a lane. A woodland path opposite parallels it left to the school's sports field, where you can carry on along the edge of the pitches below the lane. Shortly after passing beneath an impressive viaduct carrying the A36 across the valley, leave over a stile. You will find the entrance to the car park just to the left. ●

The Kennet and Avon Canal meets the Somerset Coal Canal at Dundas Bridge

11 *Crook Peak*

Although some 625 ft (190m) above sea level, the ascent of Crook Peak is not overly demanding and, on a fine day, is rewarded by a wonderful view from the summit. The return through Compton Bishop, a small hamlet in a fold below, passes an ancient church, some of its structure is considered to be by the builders of Wells Cathedral.

START Cross
DISTANCE 5½ miles (8.9km)
APPROXIMATE TIME 3 hours
PARKING Roadside parking near the White Hart Inn
ROUTE FEATURES Moderate climbs; field paths

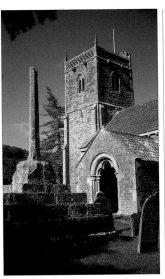

St Andrew's Church

Walk some 200 yds west of the White Hart Inn to find a marked footpath between the houses on the right. It climbs away beside a hedge, crossing a stile into a disused quarry. Go left to a ladder-stile and then bear

? Look for the churchwarden's chest in St Andrew's Church. How many old locks does it have and why?

PUBLIC TRANSPORT Bus service from Weston-super-Mare
REFRESHMENTS White Hart Inn
ORDNANCE SURVEY MAPS Explorer 153 (Weston-super-Mare & Bleadon Hill), Landranger 182 (Weston-super-Mare)

right across pasture past an indented corner to a kissing-gate. Keeping the hedge on your left, walk along the bottom of the ensuing fields, eventually reaching a narrow lane below Bourton Farm **(A)**.

Go up to its end and turn left in front of the farmhouse. Through a gate, turn right to climb a grass swathe. Pass through the left-hand gate at the top of the field and follow the ongoing path through bracken and bramble straight up the hill into Bourton Coombe, keeping left where it forks higher up. Towards the top, as the gradient eases, keep straight on to Hill Farm.

At a waypost in front of it **(B)** turn left on a broad track rising beside a wall along Wavering Down. Another strenuous climb takes you to a triangulation pillar on the top of the hill. Carry on beside the wall, the path now pleasantly undulating along the broad ridge over the lesser top of Compton

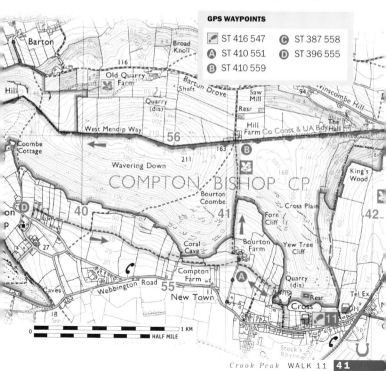

GPS WAYPOINTS

🖉 ST 416 547		**C**	ST 387 558
A	ST 410 551	**D**	ST 396 555
B	ST 410 559		

Hill. It eventually falls to a shallow saddle where the wall ends.

The path to the top of Crook Peak **C** lies ahead, the last few yards of the direct ascent presenting an easy scramble, but which can be avoided by a short detour around the side.

Return to the corner of the wall and now go right, taking the waymarked footpath rather than the parallel bridleway that leaves just before it.

Head into a deepening fold, lower down leaving the open hill into a tunnel of interlocking stunted trees. Ignore a path off left and then a crossing bridlepath, beyond which the path broadens to a grass strip below woodland. Nearing the village, fork right onto a narrower path, which runs within the tree fringe. Keep going beside the boundary, the way eventually turning down to meet another path. Go left through a gate and wind down to the end of a lane. Walk to a junction and turn left to St Andrew's Church.

Bend right before the church but at the next junction **D**, take the track ahead. Swing right at the top, passing behind gardens into a stable yard. Over a stile beside a gate, continue at the edge of successive fields. Later approaching a house, skirt left around its garden and carry on to meet the narrow lane below Bourton Farm **A**. Cross and reverse your outward steps back to the village.

Cheddar Reservoir from Wavering Down

The Saxons gave the name **Compton** to the village; with 'Bishop' added later when the bishops of Wells held the manor. Parts of St Andrew's Church, the south doorway and font, are 12th century. Many of the pews have a door, but those at the back and along the north aisle do not and are labelled 'free'. Nineteenth-century refurbishment grants often carried a condition that some seats remain 'free', in days when affluent church-goers 'rented' their private pews.

Priddy and its burial mounds

START Priddy
DISTANCE 4¾ miles (6.8km)
APPROXIMATE TIME 2 hours
PARKING Roadside parking around Priddy Green
ROUTE FEATURES Moderate climb; field paths; quiet lanes without footpaths

12

Prehistoric farmers settled the Mendips, and enigmatic traces of their presence lie scattered throughout the hills. However, nowhere are they more spectacularly concentrated than around Priddy, where numerous barrows corrugate the skyline of North Hill. To reach them, the walk passes old lead mines, whose abandoned hollows and spoil heaps are now an important wildlife habitat.

🖊 Head north up a lane beside Manor Farm, which overlooks the green. Bear off right through a barrier along a drive to the church and then turn right in front of the adjacent school. Priddy is the highest village in Somerset, with its church, St Laurence's, standing even higher. Inside, stone benches line the walls, seats for the old and sick in a time before there were pews and the congregation stood to hear the service.

Beyond the school cross a stile Ⓐ, and walk ahead to the farthest corner of the field, where it

The hurdle stack at Priddy

PUBLIC TRANSPORT None
REFRESHMENTS Pubs in Priddy
ORDNANCE SURVEY MAPS Explorer 141 (Cheddar Gorge & Mendip Hills West), Landranger 182 (Weston-super-Mare)

narrows to a point. Over a stile, keep going in the same direction, making for another stile, to the right of a gate on the far boundary. Climb beside a wall in the next field and, through a gate at the top, bear right. From a ladder-stile, head towards Eastwater Farm and

into a caravan field. Turn right past the farm buildings and walk out to East Water Lane **B**.

Some 50 yds along to the right, pass through a gate on the left and bear right, walking the length of

GPS WAYPOINTS

	ST 527 510	**C**	ST 544 507
A	ST 528 513	**D**	ST 539 515
B	ST 537 508	**E**	ST 539 523

Keep your eyes open on the way to Priddy church to discover when the first pure water supply was installed in the village.

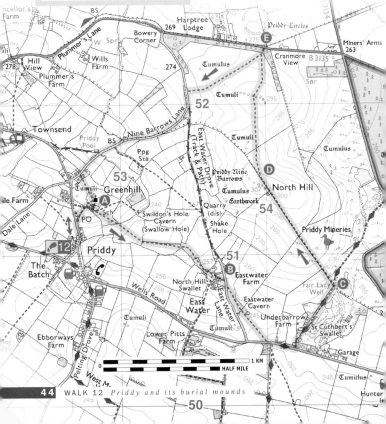

the next couple of fields. A deepening gully over to the left abruptly terminates at a sinkhole, Eastwater Cavern. Continue beyond to leave the field onto a lane, Wells Road, and turn left.

After passing a couple of cottages, go left on a track to Underbarrow Farm. Where it bends, walk ahead, signed 'Priddy Pool', in front of a building and on over a stile onto a track. Cross a second stile opposite and then follow an undulating path beside the overgrown site of old lead workings. Farther on, the way

Known as **Priddy Mineries**, the area was once extensively worked for its lead ore, perhaps since Roman times. Because of lead contamination, the land is now unsuitable for grazing, and nature has been left to re-colonise the old spoil heaps and pits. The site is now a nature reserve and home to many species, particularly plants, reptiles and invertebrates.

runs beneath trees, bringing you to a crossing of paths under a large beech tree **C**.

Go left, loosely following a wall up the edge of rough ground onto North Hill. At the top, cross a stile into a meadow and progress beside the wall past Priddy Nine Barrows.

After passing the final prominent mound of the first group **D** bear right to a stile and continue across the next field. Two more barrows stand to the left and, in front, a whole herd of them graze the

Priddy Pool and the surrounding land provide a valuable nature reserve

Some of the barrows above Priddy

In the field to the left, at the top of North Hill, lie a string of Bronze Age burial mounds, known as **Priddy Nine Barrows**. Six of them are particularly prominent, forming a dramatic sequence along the horizon. None is open, so resist climbing the wall into the adjacent field.

skyline. Pass between them and carry on to a gate by a break in the trees at the far side of the field **E**. Cross the road and look towards Priddy Circles, four earthwork enclosures that stand in a line, slightly east of due north. Each is about 180 yards in diameter and defined by a low bank and shallow ditch.

Return to the field and bear right to walk past the right end of the barrows. Leave by a gate onto Nine Barrows Lane and go left. After ½ mile, just beyond a cottage on the left, turn down beside it and go through a gate into a field. Head towards the church, walking past it to reach the drive beyond **A**.

Reverse your outward route back to the village green, where you will see the famous Priddy Hurdles stored under a thatch. They were used for the annual sheep fair, which still takes place in August. However, today, new hurdles are brought in for the occasion to avoid having to dismantle the stack. ●

The hills above Nether Stowey

13

START Nether Stowey

DISTANCE 5½ miles (8.9km)

APPROXIMATE TIME 3 hours

PARKING Car park by library and Quantocks AONB Office

ROUTE FEATURES Moderate climbs, woodland and field paths, quiet lanes without footpaths

This delightful walk begins in the picturesque village of Nether Stowey, where the poet Samuel Taylor Coleridge spent the closing years of the 18th century. It climbs onto the wooded fringes of the Quantocks and visits two 'castles' built in different ages, both occupying commanding hilltops that offer outstanding views over the surrounding countryscape.

Walk up Castle Street and keep ahead at a junction, signed Over Stowey. Ignore side streets, but bear left at a fork to pass below the castle mound, which then rises on your right. You will see it again at the end of the walk.

Beyond the crest, the lane shortly drops to a T-junction **A**, where you should go left. After roughly

Although trees now cover most of **Dowsborough**, it was a bare hill when Iron Age defences were thrown up around its summit. The arboreal cover now obscures the surrounding embankments, but the view north is spectacular evidence of the commanding position it held.

150 yds turn off onto a bridleway that climbs to the right. Shortly, after following a stream, a stile on the right takes the path above the water-course. Rejoining the stream higher up, the way soon emerges onto a lane beside a cottage **B**. Turn left, ford the stream and climb away. Just after a barn and cottage, take a track on the right that rises across open fields.

PUBLIC TRANSPORT Bus service from Bridgwater

REFRESHMENTS Pubs and tearoom in Nether Stowey

PUBLIC TOILETS Adjacent to car park

ORDNANCE SURVEY MAPS Explorer 140 (Quantock Hills & Bridgwater), Landranger 181 (Minehead & Brendon Hills)

Higher up, where it bends left between two large white boulders, bear right through a gate into a field. Continue with the fence on the left to another gate, just beyond the crest. Through that, walk ahead to the top-right corner, where a gate on the right leads into a wood **C**.

> **?** *What is the most common woodland tree on Dowsborough Hill?*

Follow the path ahead beside an ancient, outgrown beech hedge for about 150 yds to a waymarked crossing. There, turn right; the path then undulates and twists through oak and beech wood interspersed by more open areas of bracken and shrub-clad heathland. After some ¾ mile the path ends at a lane.

Walk up the hill for 150 yds before bearing off right along a rising banked path into the woodland above the road. When you reach a crossing of paths **D**, turn right to climb Dowsborough Hill. Go forward at the next junction and take the left fork higher up, the ascent becoming more determined. Reaching a crossing track, go left, the gradient easing as you broach the crest of the hill. The way crosses and follows the encircling earthwork of the hillfort, shortly breaking into a small clearing **E**.

A clear path drops to the right, descending across open gorse and heather heath. At a waymarked junction, turn sharp right and contour below the oaken top of the hill. Later pass back into the woodland, at first birch and then beech, some of the oldest trees in the wood. You eventually emerge onto a lane. Turn down the hill to a sharp bend at Walford's Gibbet **F**, named after a forest charcoal-burner, John Walford, whose body

Stowey Castle was built by the Normans in the 11th century, a simple motte-and-bailey, that is, a central keep on a mound surrounded by an enclosed court. Although it was demolished some 400 years later, and the stone taken away for use in the construction of nearby Stowey Court, the earthwork and embankments remain a prominent feature.

was strung up there for a year after he was hanged for the murder of his wife.

Leave the lane at this point, going ahead through a gate to walk down an open field, shortly joining a descending boundary. Lower down, leave through a gate onto a hedged track and go left down to Hack Lane. Follow that right for about ¼ mile.

Just beyond the crest of the hill, cross a waymarked stile through the hedge on the left **G**. Walk downfield, initially beside the left-hand hedge and continuing beyond its end; ahead is Stowey Castle. Over a stile at the bottom, turn left along a lane but then immediately walk right onto a track below the castle. A few yards along, go right over the second of two adjacent

Sheep wandering through the woods

stiles and climb to the earthwork surrounding the central mound. The final ascent appears formidable, but an easy way up can be found on the far side.

Drop through the southern defences out onto a lane. The village and car park are down the hill to the left. ●

GPS WAYPOINTS

🖉 ST 190 396	**D** ST 162 388
A ST 184 393	**E** ST 159 392
B ST 177 393	**F** ST 173 394
C ST 174 387	**G** ST 182 395

14 Around Fyne Court and Broomfield

START	Fyne Court (National Trust)
DISTANCE	3½ miles (5.6km)
APPROXIMATE TIME	1½ hours
PARKING	Car park at start
ROUTE FEATURES	Woodland and field paths; quiet lanes without footpaths

Beginning at Fyne Court, which houses the Quantocks Visitor Centre; this walk explores some of the rich woodland cloaking the deep river valleys that cleave the south-eastern corner of the Quantocks. There is much to look for among the trees, and the return along the top of the valley offers fine views across the hills to the south.

Return to the road outside the car park and walk left towards Broomfield church. Before you reach it, however, turn right over a waymarked stile and go through a gate into a paddock. Walk directly downhill to a double ranch stile and continue descending the subsequent field. Go right along the bottom boundary to find a stile leading on to a track by Rosegate Kennels Ⓐ.

Cross to another stile opposite and climb the open field beside its fence. At the crest of the hill, go through a gate on the right. Now bear left, crossing a stile hidden in the far hedge to emerge onto a lane. Walk down some 50 yds, passing a junction, and then go left, dropping quite steeply along a hedged track into Wort Wood.

Only the library and music room survive from the 17th-century **Fyne Court** that was all but destroyed by a fire in 1894. It was the home of the Crosse family, of whom the best-remembered member is Andrew. A philosopher and gentleman scientist, he was a pioneer in the study of electricity during the early 19th century. Local people christened him the 'Thunder and Lightning Man', because of the eerie flashes of light and explosive crashes that emanated from his workshops late into the night.

PUBLIC TRANSPORT None
REFRESHMENTS Tearoom and picnic area at Fyne Court
PUBLIC TOILETS Fyne Court Visitor Centre
ORDNANCE SURVEY MAPS Explorer 140 (Quantock Hills & Bridgwater), Landranger 182 (Weston-super-Mare)

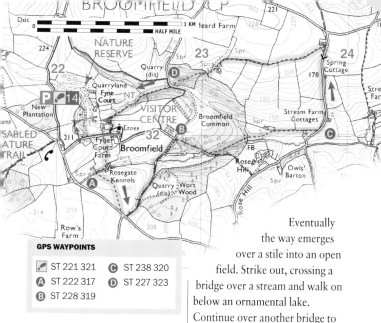

GPS WAYPOINTS

📍 ST 221 321	**C** ST 238 320
A ST 222 317	**D** ST 227 323
B ST 228 319	

Over a stream at the bottom, climb on through the trees to reach a junction of tracks at the corner of a lane **B**.

Ignore the track immediately right; instead cross and then go right, along a path waymarked 'Quantock Greenway'. It falls back into the woods, shortly meeting the stream you crossed earlier. However, instead of fording it, turn left onto an initially indistinct path, following the course of the stream.

Eventually the way emerges over a stile into an open field. Strike out, crossing a bridge over a stream and walk on below an ornamental lake. Continue over another bridge to cross a stile, and there bear left uphill to follow the top border of the field. Keep the same heading

> **?** Who do you suppose carved the bench ends of the pews in Broomfield church?

Young enthusiasts at Fyne Court Visitor Centre

through a couple of gates and on past a wooded garden to leave onto a lane. Take care, for the path drops directly onto the carriageway **C**.

To the left, the lane climbs steeply away, eventually reaching some cottages near the top. Turn left onto a track immediately before them and follow it across the fields above the valley. Farther along, the way twists through a hedge, continuing on its opposite side. Gently descending and shortly narrowing to a path, it ultimately emerges into the corner of a field. Keep ahead alongside an overgrown hedge to a stile beyond a massive old beech tree.

Back in woodland, follow a winding and occasionally indistinct path through the trees, dropping to cross a stream. Above the

opposite bank, a more evident path leads left, soon losing height to a lane **D**.

Cross to a gate opposite, from which a track rises beside a wood along a shallow, open valley. Keep going to the top of the fields and continue climbing on a wooded track that ends at a gate into a field. Walk on at the edge, leaving through a final gate on the right to reach a lane beside the church. Turn right and walk back to the starting point at Fyne Court. ●

Inside the **Church of St Mary and All Saints** beneath the tower and protected by a mat is a brass effigy. It shows Richard Dulverton, a 15th-century priest of the church, clad in his mass vestments. The carved bench ends of the pews are also impressive for the variety and fineness of the carvings that adorn them.

A green lane follows the hills above Broomfield

The Parrett between Langport and Muchelney Abbey

START River Parrett Visitor Centre, Langport

DISTANCE 4 miles (6.4km)

APPROXIMATE TIME 1½ hours

PARKING Car park at Visitor Centre

ROUTE FEATURES Riverside paths (occasionally impassable after prolonged rain), quiet lanes without footpaths

15

Langport was once a prosperous seaport dealing in trade from the East Indies. Across the marsh lies Muchelney, a low island that was settled by monks in the 8th century, although the ruins are of a later abbey, which was founded around 950.

A bridge behind the Visitor Centre leads to a footpath on the Parrett's opposite bank. Follow it upstream beside the river for a little over ½ mile to a confluence with the Yeo at Huish Bridge **A**.

Cross over and resume your progress upstream, the path signed to Muchelney. Keep going at the

> **?** What is the symbol marking the Parrett Trail on the way to Muchelney Abbey?

The abbot's lodgings and ruins of the abbey church

PUBLIC TRANSPORT Bus service from Bridgwater

REFRESHMENTS Pubs in Langport, tearoom at Muchelney, picnic area by Visitor Centre

PUBLIC TOILETS Adjacent to Visitor Centre

ORDNANCE SURVEY MAPS Explorer 129 (Yeovil & Sherborne), Landranger 193 (Taunton & Lyme Regis)

edge of successive fields until, eventually, you emerge at Westover Bridge **B**. Turn left and follow a lane into Muchelney. You pass behind the abbey ruins as you approach the village, but keep going to a junction by the village green. As you bend right in front of the church, the Priest's House then lies on your left. Continue along

the lane to reach the entrance to the abbey **C**.

Leave the village by the same lane you came in on, but continue along it past Westover Bridge

Following its destruction by Danish raiders, **Muchelney Abbey** was refounded in the 10th century and survived until the Dissolution. The abbot's lodgings continued in use for another 400 years as a secular residence. Despite its isolation, Muchelney Abbey became wealthy. The 14th-century Bishop of Wells was not impressed with the monks' lavish ways and commanded a return to the austerities and disciplines of their Benedictine foundation. He also ordered the rebuilding of the adjacent parish church and the provision of a residence for its priest.

GPS WAYPOINTS

ST 415 265	**C**	ST 429 248
A ST 424 263	**D**	ST 422 247
B ST 424 248		

The **Priest's House** is an attractive building with stone mullioned windows and a gothic doorway, and stands at the heart of the hamlet behind a wonderful country garden. The bishop required the abbot to maintain the parish priest with a daily allowance of bread and ale as well as fish or eggs, with meat being substituted on Sundays and Tuesdays.

B, the way lined by pollarded willows. Beyond the buttresses of a dismantled bridge **D**, double back to the right and pass through a couple of gates onto the course of an abandoned railway, signed as the Langport and Parrett Cycleway. The railway was one of those that fell under Dr Beeching's axe after his controversial report in 1963.

The main line still runs through Langport to the north, but its station too has been closed.

Follow its raised course across the flood meadows to Langport. Through a gate at the end, turn right and then left to bypass a small business area. Continue ahead along a road back to the Visitor Centre. ●

Enter **Muchelney's church** and its painted roof immediately strikes you, executed in the 1600s, it depicts angels, looking more worldly than heavenly dressed in Tudor high fashion. The floor tiles below the altar were rescued from the abbey's lady chapel – look for elephants and knights on horseback. The 19th-century organ is also a rare survival.

The 14th-century Priest's House

16 *Ham Hill and Montacute*

START Ham Hill Country Park
DISTANCE 4½ miles (7.2km)
APPROXIMATE TIME 2 hours
PARKING Norton car park
ROUTE FEATURES Woodland and field paths, moderate climbs

From the number of houses, halls and churches built of Ham stone, it is a wonder there is any hill left, but at some 450ft (137m) high, Ham Hill remains a fine vantage. To the east, beyond St Michael's Hill lies Montacute, an attractive village with a fine Elizabethan house.

Stone Age tribes visited **Ham Hill** long before Iron Age people built a massive fort here, one of the largest in Europe. You can still see remains of its ditch and rampart defences. It was the Romans who began the quarrying of the beautiful honey-coloured limestone, an activity that continues today.

Diagonally opposite the car park, a path winds left between grassed hillocks to the ranger station. Follow the drive left to a junction and go right towards the Prince of Wales. However, leave immediately through a gate on the

Early morning mist at Montacute

PUBLIC TRANSPORT Bus service from Yeovil to Montacute (alternative start)
REFRESHMENTS Pubs and tearooms in Montacute, pub and picnic area at Ham Hill
CHILDREN'S PLAY AREA Beside route at Montacute
PUBLIC TOILETS Ham Hill Country Park and Montacute
ORDNANCE SURVEY MAPS Explorer 129 (Yeovil & Sherborne), Landranger 193 (Taunton & Lyme Regis)

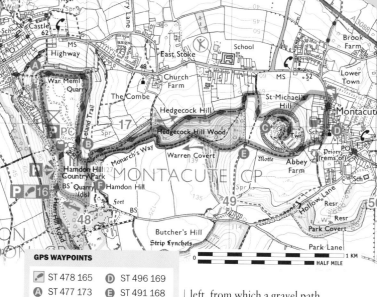

GPS WAYPOINTS

🖊 ST 478 165		**D** ST 496 169	
A ST 477 173		**E** ST 491 168	
B ST 479 168		**F** ST 480 166	
C ST 492 170			

St Michael's Tower

left, from which a gravel path contours the flank of the hill.

A view soon opens across the countryside, a topograph farther on identifying some of the landmarks. Carry on to the war memorial **A** from which the extent of the ancient hillfort is visible, its outer rampart encircling later quarries.

Continue along the ridge-top path, looking ahead to St Michael's Hill. Farther round, a break in the embankment is possibly an early

> **?** *How many steps make the staircase up the tower on St Michael's Hill?*

Montacute House

giving views back to Ham Hill.

Watch for steps descending to a lower path, which continues pleasantly around the wooded northern flank of Hedgecock Hill. Ignore side paths, later passing a ruined pump house. Approaching the eastern end of the wood, swing left past a junction and then right before the entrance to a farm. At the next bend, leave right through a gate and head up to a stile at the foot of St Michael's Hill **C**. The climbing path ahead spirals to the top.

Return to the stile, but instead of crossing, take the hollow path right

entrance to the settlement. Regaining the earthwork, keep going to emerge near the Prince of Wales.

Go past the pub, leaving just beyond down a stepped path, signed to Montacute **B**. A few steps below, turn left through a gate and continue to the bottom. Go right through a gate to join with another path. Then, at a junction, bear left onto a bridleway, again signed to Montacute. A broad path contours the hillside

> **St Michael's Hill** also has an Iron Age fort, the path up its steep slopes passing through the still impressive earthworks. The Normans built a castle too, which particularly angered local Saxons who believed a fragment of the Holy Cross had been found there. Sir Edward Phelips of Montacute House built the tower now standing on the top as an observatory in 1760.

beside the boundary. Reaching a second stile, head down-meadow to a kissing-gate. Keep going to another kissing-gate and turn right at the edge of playing fields. Emerging onto a street, go right again into Montacute.

At a junction by St Catherine's Church , the entrance to Montacute House and the village's fascinating museum are to the left. The onward path, however, lies along the drive ahead. After 50 yds, turn right into Abbey Farm, passing through a gate at the rear of the yard. Go ahead and then left, rising beside the left boundary. Continue beyond St Michael's Hill towards Hedgecock Hill. At a crossing of paths, walk forward and over a stile into the wood , joining another path to go left. Pass right of a gate marked private and then shortly take a right fork. Keep going between the trees above a steepening bank, later glimpsing your outward path. Remain high, briefly following an overgrown wall before bearing away left to wind

The 16th-century gatehouse, now part of Abbey Farm, is almost all that remains of Montacute's 11th-century Cluniac priory. Many of its stones were incorporated in **Montacute House**, built at the end of the 16th century for Sir Edward Phelips. It is remarkable, amongst other things, for its immense gallery, 189 feet long. **St Catherine's Church** has some interesting Phelips' tombs. Have a look too at the organ loft, supported on corbels carved with musicians playing an assortment of instruments.

between the grassed hummocks of old workings.

Reaching a clearing where two sculptures have been erected ; keep ahead to join a broad path. After passing the entrance to Deep Quarry, emerge onto a lane and turn right back to the car park. ●

Ham Hill Country Park

17 Westwood Manor, Farleigh Hungerford and Iford Manor

START Westwood
DISTANCE 6¼ miles (10.1km)
APPROXIMATE TIME 3 hours
PARKING Roadside parking in Westwood
ROUTE FEATURES Field paths and quiet lanes without pavements

A 15th-century manor, ruined castle with an intriguing chapel and beautiful Italian-style gardens all compete for attention on this longer walk that explores the countryside of the Frome Valley.

Follow the lane east through the village. Some 75 yds after passing Orchard Close, look for steps to a stile on the right **A**. Cross a couple of paddocks and walk beside an overgrown hedge to a crossing path. Keep ahead into St Mary's churchyard, walking around the church to the lane beside Westwood Manor.

Cross to a stile opposite and bear right on a field trod towards Farleigh Hungerford. After passing behind a cottage, keep by the right hedge, eventually delving through

Begun in the 15th century, **Westwood Manor** is a charming house, its fabric reflecting changing styles over three centuries. It has some striking Jacobean plaster ceilings and contains a fine collection of 16th- and 17th-century furniture, including the earliest working Italian keyboard in the country. Recordings of the restored instruments add a special atmosphere while children will enjoy searching out answers to a quiz.

a small copse to emerge onto the lane. A few yards to the left, another stile takes you back into meadow. Although little more than low banks and shallow hollows are

PUBLIC TRANSPORT Bus service from Bath to Westwood
REFRESHMENTS Pub at Farleigh Hungerford, teas at Iford Manor and Stowford Farm
ORDNANCE SURVEY MAPS Explorers 142 (Chippenham & Bradford-on-Avon) and 156 (Shepton Mallet & Mendip Hills East), Landrangers 172 (Bristol & Bath) and 173 (Swindon & Devizes)

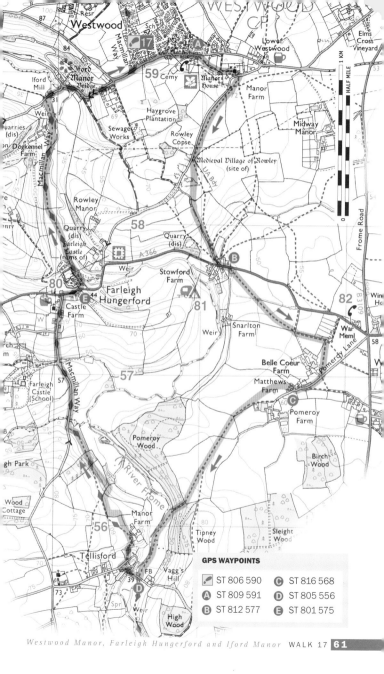

GPS WAYPOINTS

✎ ST 806 590	Ⓒ ST 816 568
Ⓐ ST 809 591	Ⓓ ST 805 556
Ⓑ ST 812 577	Ⓔ ST 801 575

Farleigh Hungerford Castle

Immediately go over a stile on the left and head out on a diagonal, aiming for a distant large barn. Cross an intervening boundary where fence meets hedge and maintain the line to the top corner of the next field. Go through the gate on the right and turn left beside the hedge. Over a stiled ditch strike half-right, crossing a final field onto Pomeroy Lane.

to be seen today, these fields were the site of an ancient village, Rowley. The earliest mention of a settlement is from 1001 and, although the village had been abandoned by the middle of the 16th century, there was still a farm here in the latter part of the 19th century. Strike a diagonal to the far corner and carry on ahead along a bounded path, where a break in the hedge reveals a view to the Westbury White Horse.

The way soon drops along a sunken lane to meet the main road at Stowford Farm. Go left but after 100 yds, take the second track off on the right **B**.

Walk right for 300 yds leaving immediately before a pair of houses through a kissing-gate on the right **C**. Head out to a second kissing-gate and bear left, parallel to a large barn and then wire fence to find a footbridge in the end hedge. Carry on, crossing a stile in a short fence breaking the hedge ahead and keep the same course across the next large pasture to its farthest tip. From a kissing-gate, a narrow path drops steeply through a wood to emerge in a meadow. Bearing left, follow the River Frome upstream, exiting at the far end onto a path at Tellisford.

Over the pretty 17th-century bridge **D** walk on past buildings and climb a cobbled path to a narrow lane beside Crabb House. Turn right and then fork left towards Manor Farm. Approaching the house, leave through a gate on the left. Head away on a grass track at the field edge. Passing into the next field, swing up left. However, instead of continuing through the next gap, turn right along the top edge of the field. At the far side, go through a small gate and walk down to a field gate. Pass through a rough clearing flanked by trees, shortly entering the wood. Leaving the trees, walk the length of a long meadow to meet a lane. Turn right and follow it over the hill to Farleigh Hungerford, passing Farleigh House, which lies across the fields to the left.

Reaching the main road, the pub lies just to the left, but the route is to the right. Walk down and cross to a small parking area by the entrance to Farleigh Hungerford Castle **E**. A stepped path drops below the castle to meet a track. Go left but where it bends after 50 yds, branch off across grass to a footbridge. Emerging beyond a copse by the river the path continues across meadows. Again closing with the river, keep going until you ultimately reach a kissing-gate onto a lane.

> **?** *Who is standing on the bridge overlooking the River Frome at Iford?*

Go right, walking down to Iford Bridge. At a junction in front of the entrance to Iford Manor, turn right, climbing steeply beside the walled gardens. During the first part of the 20th century, the manor was the home of the renowned architect and landscape gardener Harold Peto. He created the wonderful Italianate gardens for which the house is now known. They are open during the summer months. Reaching the top, turn right back to Westwood. ●

Originally a manor house, **Farleigh Hungerford Castle** was first fortified around 1370 by Sir Thomas Hungerford, the House of Commons' first Speaker. His son, Sir William extended the defences some 50 years later to incorporate an outer court, and it is largely his work that survives today. Some impressive parts of the defences remain, and the chapel contains beautiful wall paintings, fine stained glass and some amazing tombs of the Hungerford family.

● Neolithic burial mound ● 14th-century church ● extensive views

18 *Wellow to Stony Littleton*

START	Wellow
DISTANCE	6 miles (9.7km)
APPROXIMATE TIME	3 hours
PARKING	Car park in Station Road
ROUTE FEATURES	Moderate climb, field paths and farm tracks, remember a torch to explore the barrow

The walk's highlight is undoubtedly the fine Neolithic barrow above Stony Littleton, which occupies a commanding hillside position overlooking Wellow Brook. However, other attractions are the fine views over the surrounding countryside and the diversity of wildflowers that grow in the hedgerows. Wellow's church, at the eastern end of the village, is also worth a visit.

🖊 From the car park, return to the main street and go right into the village. When you reach a junction near the Fox and Badger, turn left. About 150 yds up the hill, leave over a waymarked stile to the left beside the gateway of a house. Walk on through a gate and, maintaining a diagonal line up the hillside, climb across the fields until, eventually, you emerge over a final stile onto a track along the top of the hill **A**.

Follow the track to the left. There is a wonderful view across the valley. On the opposite hillside, you can see the prominent mound

Relaxing in Wellow

PUBLIC TRANSPORT None
REFRESHMENTS Fox and Badger in Wellow
ORDNANCE SURVEY MAPS Explorer 142 (Shepton Mallet & Mendip Hills East), Landranger 172 (Bristol & Bath)

The entrance to Stoney Littleton Long Barrow

of Stoney Littleton Long Barrow, which is visited later in the walk.

During the early centuries of the first millennium, this part of England became **'Romanised'**. The countryside was extensively farmed, with estates centred on substantial villas, the comfortable homes of the wealthy landowners. Although no obvious sign remains, one such villa was discovered on the hillside west of Wellow. The well-drained, southward-facing slopes that surrounded it could well have been exploited for the cultivation of vines, something that is still practised in parts of the county today.

Where the way forks, bear left and keep going for a further ½ mile, gently losing height before reaching a junction of tracks **B**.

Go left and walk down to Bourne Farm, continuing ahead through the farmyard and out to a lane beyond, Wellow Road. To the right, it winds steeply downhill to Double Hill Farm at the bottom of the valley **C**.

Turn left into the farmyard there and go through a gate beside the barns into a field, seemingly designated a cemetery for defunct agricultural equipment. Follow the hedge on the left through successive fields. Cross straight over when you reach a hedged

? *How many burial chambers lead off the passage in Stoney Littleton Long Barrow?*

Horse riders in Wellow village

footbridge but instead of crossing, walk past it to a stile. Continue up beside the hedge to another stile and turn left, signed 'Stoney Littleton Barrow'. Go right at the next stile and climb to the mound **E**.

A path across the field from near the mouth of the chamber leads back to a track along the top of the field by a hedge.

track, Brinscombe Lane, and keep going along the subsequent fields beside a stream that flows at the base of the hedge. Eventually, the stream falls away below you through a rough paddock. Keep ahead to reach a crossing track at the bottom of the final field. Turn right and walk out to a lane **D**.

To the left, the lane drops over Wellow Brook, rising again to a track leading to Stony Littleton Manor Farm. Keep going through the farmyard and leave by a gate into the field beyond. A little farther on, bear left towards a

Stoney Littleton Long Barrow is an impressive funerary monument for high-ranking individuals and served as a focal point for the local tribe over many generations. People of the New Stone Age culture built it about 5,000 years ago, some 500 years before the Egyptians embarked upon the construction of their Great Pyramid at Giza.

There is a long tradition of Christianity at Wellow and there may even have been a Romano-Christian church here. **St Julian's Church** is presumed to date from around 1370, constructed by Sir Thomas of Farleigh Hungerford. Inside, the impressive wooden roof is carried on corbels, carved as angels, and a magnificent screen separates the nave from the chancel. The Hungerford Chapel contains funerary monuments and on the wall are beautiful 15th-century frescoes.

Turn left and follow it, eventually losing height to a lane at its end. There, go left, descending to a ford and bridge over Wellow Brook. Continue up to a crossroads in the village. St Julian's Church lies a short way to the right, while the car park is to the left.

GPS WAYPOINTS

	ST 738 580	**C**	ST 718 572
A	ST 728 584	**D**	ST 725 565
B	ST 715 576	**E**	ST 735 572

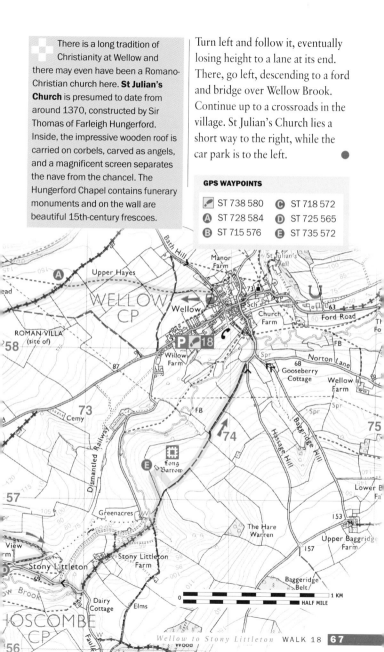

19 *Great Elm and Mells*

START Great Elm

DISTANCE 5 miles (8km)

TIME 2½ hours

PARKING Lay-by above river

ROUTE FEATURES River banks, woodland and field paths, short section along busy road

Two deep, steep-sided valleys converge below the hamlet of Great Elm, each harbouring fast-flowing streams in the dense woodland foliage that cloaks their sides. This longer walk explores something of both, punctuated by a wander through the charming village of Mells where there is an ancient church. The way back passes the substantial overgrown ruins of a former ironworks.

From the road, just above the south bank of Mells River, a track leaves into the woods that line its upstream bank. However, instead of following the track ahead, immediately through the gate, go left up a narrow path into the trees. When you reach a track at the top, turn right and follow the edge of the wood for ½ mile, eventually emerging left onto a road Ⓐ.

Cross to a gate opposite, from which a grass path leads forward into a field. Continue beside its left-hand hedge to the corner. Ignore the gate ahead and, instead, go right along a tree-lined path.

The entrance to the village lock-up at Mells

PUBLIC TRANSPORT Bus service from Frome to Mells (alternative start)

REFRESHMENTS Talbot Inn and teas at walled garden in Mells

ORDNANCE SURVEY MAPS Explorer 142 (Shepton Mallet & Mendip Hills East), Landranger 183 (Yeovil & Frome)

Feeding ducks by the river at Great Elm

At the bottom, pass into a field on the left and walk on beside the right boundary, once again at the edge of woodland above Fordbury Water. Keep ahead along successive fields, until a final gate takes the stepped way down a wooded bank onto the road **B**.

Take care along the busy road, which, to the right, drops into the valley and past the vehicle exit from the Whatley limestone quarry. Continue up the hill and, shortly after passing the quarry's upper entrance, leave over a waymarked stile on the left. A footpath parallels the road below a steep, wooded embankment, which screens the limestone quarry workings.

Emerging from the trees, carry on along a broad green swathe that then swings left. Eventually, the path diverges from the road, following a line of overhead power cables. Some 20 yds after passing the fenced corner of a wood on your left and before reaching a junction of power cables, bear half-right to a boulder protruding from the grass. Pass through trees beside a house and head down a rough meadow to its far-right corner behind a bungalow. Leave over a stile onto a lane **C**.

Cross to another stile opposite. Follow the right-hand hedge to a gap, slipping through to continue with the hedge on your left. Mounting a stile, walk out to a

Before the Dissolution, the manor of **Mells** was part of the Glastonbury Abbey estates. In the late 15th century, John Selwood, then abbot, embarked on a rebuilding plan to create a 'model village'. He got no further than New Street, the road beside the Talbot Inn leading to the church, before events overtook him. The estate was acquired by the Horner family, its former bailiffs under the abbot. However, there is no evidence that they employed the skulduggery implied by the nursery rhyme *Little Jack Horner*.

lane. Turn right but almost immediately bear off right again, along a path falling through trees to another lane. Go right and then fork left to cross Mells Stream. Carry on, branching left at a fork to reach the main village street, opposite the entrance to the manor. Turn right and walk through the village to New Street **D**, which leads to the church.

Continue along the main street, bearing right by the war memorial to the next junction. Ignore the left turn immediately after the post office and, instead, fork left just beyond. After 300 yds, abandon it for a bridleway on the right **E**, which winds into a narrow,

GPS WAYPOINTS

✐ ST 748 491	**C** ST 724 486
A ST 745 484	**D** ST 727 492
B ST 732 477	**E** ST 733 490

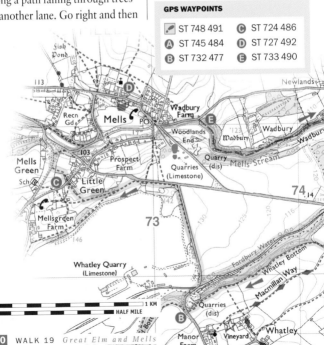

wooded gorge that contains Mells Stream.

You do not have to walk far before encountering crumbling and overgrown walls. Now half-hidden by encroaching vegetation, they were built for an iron industry that filled this cramped valley. The main concentration of ruins lies a little farther on, to the right where the path forks.

? *Who stands on top of the column above the war memorial in Mells and what is he doing?*

After exploring the ruins, return to the fork and take the other branch. It rises behind the main buildings before returning to the riverbank lower down. Eventually, the track joins a tarmac drive.

A short distance farther on, watch for a path bearing off right across a grass clearing. Passing back into woodland, continue by the river to a footbridge. Cross

Fussells Iron Works was famous for the production of fine tools. Both the iron ore and limestone needed for its smelting were mined nearby and brought here, where the stream provided the power needed to drive furnace bellows and forging hammers. *Be careful if you explore the ruins, for there are hidden holes where the river still gushes beneath.*

and continue downstream on the opposite bank to meet a joining stream, Fordbury Water. Cross a bridge to the right and turn left. A wide track then leads back to the road at Great Elm.

A shelter designed by Edward Lutyens

20 Cheddar Gorge and Velvet Bottom

START	Cheddar
DISTANCE	6½ miles (10.5km)
APPROXIMATE TIME	3½ hours
PARKING	Cliff Street (Pay and Display)
ROUTE FEATURES	Steep climbs; woodland and rocky paths (may be slippery after rain); unguarded cliff edges

The great chasm of Cheddar Gorge is one of the country's most dramatic and well-known natural formations, its spectacular caves drawing visitors across the world. However, few have discovered its continuation, Velvet Bottom. Beyond a disused quarry, lies a now-quiet and beautiful valley, once the scene of activity as it was mined for lead ore.

It is thought that **Cheddar Gorge** was formed during the Ice Ages. Torrents of summer melt-waters, unabsorbed by the permafrosted limestone, cascaded off the Mendip plateau exploiting a weakness to gouge out a canyon-like valley. The caves, on the other hand, were created by water gradually dissolving the stone, as it slowly percolated through cracks in the solid rock. In turn, the evaporation of the lime-rich water dripping through underground voids or trickling over rocks created the fantastic stalactites and stalagmites and other formations.

Turn right from the car park past a mini-roundabout and take the second left, The Bays. At the end, bear left on a stepped path behind the Waterfall Restaurant. Rejoining the main road, go left and immediately sharp left before the Toy Museum along a track. After 50 yds climb steps right to a gate, waymarked 'National Trust Gorge Walk'. Head up into a wood, where a path climbs steeply along a tree-packed gully. In time, the gradient eases and the path breaks into a clearing. Walk on

PUBLIC TRANSPORT Bus service from Weston-super-Mare
REFRESHMENTS Pubs and cafés in Cheddar
PUBLIC TOILETS At car park
ORDNANCE SURVEY MAPS Explorer 141 (Cheddar Gorge & Mendip Hills West), Landranger 182 (Weston-super-Mare)

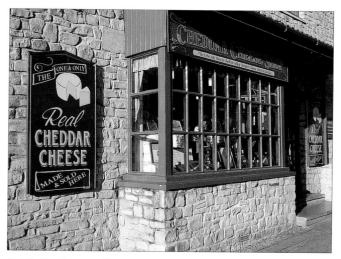

Real Cheddar cheese on offer at Cheddar Gorge

through a gate at the top to a crossing track Ⓐ and turn right.

The route ignores side and crossing tracks, but two sensational viewpoints lie off the onward path. The first is met a few yards on, to the right, over a wall. The second vantage is passed later, over a stile on the right. Farther on, keep ahead over a stile, where the trees thin to give a panoramic vista across the gorge. Eventually, after another stile, the way begins to fall, steepening and finally descending steps to a wall-stile. Over that, a path crosses a grassy bank to a wood and over another stile. The way now winds down through the

Pick up a piece of the black, glassy rubble from the slagheaps in Velvet Bottom and weigh it in your hand against a similar-sized ordinary stone. What do you notice?

trees, finally dropping to a broad track at Black Rock.

To the left, the track leads past a limekiln and below a cliff, once quarried for its stone. A little farther on, as the track leaves the National Trust Black Rock Reserve, go through a kissing-gate on the right into the Velvet Bottom Reserve Ⓑ.

Lead was mined in **Velvet Bottom** before the Romans arrived, but the most intensive periods of working were during the Roman occupation and in medieval times. The mines were finally abandoned in the 1880s, and nature has since begun to reclaim the land. It is a slow process, for few plants can tolerate the still high lead levels in the soil of the valley floor. A leaflet, available at the entrance to the reserve, describes some of the plants and insects to look out for.

and rabbit tracks may sometimes appear confusing, continue on the main path above the valley. After ½ mile, look for a waymark fixed to a hawthorn bush on the left. In a partial

Walk ahead up the base of the valley, rising through the terraces of former ore settling pits. The way winds past buddle pits used for washing the ore and then bare, black mounds of slag, the residue of the smelting process. Just past a wooden hut, which you will shortly see to the left, look for a stile across the wall on the right. Climb the valley side to reach an enclosed wood at the top, near Warren Farm **C**.

Turn right along the edge of the wood, over a stile below the farm and on to join a track dropping from it. Keep ahead, roughly parallel to a wall that lies to the left. The way gently loses height and, although the array of sheep

clearing just beyond, go right down a shallow gully and follow the wall around at the bottom to a gate, back at the foot of Velvet Bottom **B**. (If you miss the gully, the path soon peters out in bracken at the top of a rocky outcrop.)

Turn left and follow the drove back past the quarry and limekiln, continuing through a gate and eventually onto the road at the head of Cheddar Gorge **D**. Cross to a path opposite, which climbs steeply through the trees on a right diagonal. Through a gate at the

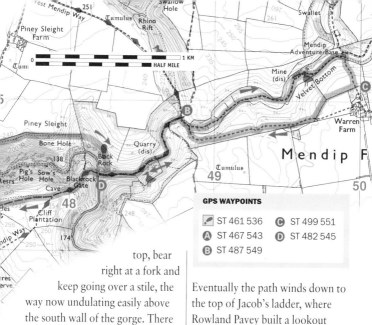

GPS WAYPOINTS

🖊 ST 461 536		**C** ST 499 551
A ST 467 543		**D** ST 482 545
B ST 487 549		

top, bear right at a fork and keep going over a stile, the way now undulating easily above the south wall of the gorge. There are a couple of places where superb views open over the gorge, but *do not get too close to the edge, for it is a long, long way down.*

Eventually the path winds down to the top of Jacob's ladder, where Rowland Pavey built a lookout tower in 1920. Complete the walk by descending the long flight of 274 steps back to the bottom of the gorge.

Black Rock used to be quarried for limestone

Further Information

Walking Safety

Although the reasonably gentle countryside that is the subject of this book offers no real dangers to walkers at any time of the year, it is still advisable to take sensible precautions and follow certain well-tried guidelines.

Always take with you both warm and waterproof clothing and sufficient food and drink. Wear suitable footwear, such as strong walking boots or shoes that give a good grip over stony ground, on slippery slopes and in muddy conditions. Try to obtain a local weather forecast and bear it in mind before you start. Do not be afraid to abandon your proposed route and return to your starting point in the event of a sudden and unexpected deterioration in the weather.

All the walks described in this book will be safe to do, given due care and respect, even during the winter. Indeed, a crisp, fine winter day often provides perfect walking conditions, with firm ground underfoot and a clarity unique to this time of the year.

The most difficult hazard likely to be encountered is mud, especially when walking along woodland and field paths, farm tracks and bridleways – the latter in particular

Open fields below Walford's Gibbet

can often get churned up by cyclists and horses. In summer, an additional difficulty may be narrow and overgrown paths, particularly along the edges of cultivated fields. Neither should constitute a major problem provided that the appropriate footwear is worn.

Follow the Country Code

- Enjoy the countryside and respect its life and work
- Guard against all risk of fire
- Take your litter home
- Fasten all gates
- Help to keep all water clean
- Keep your dogs under control
- Protect wildlife, plants and trees
- Keep to public paths across farmland
- Take special care on country roads
- Leave livestock, crops and machinery alone
- Make no unnecessary noise
- Use gates and stiles to cross fences, hedges and walls
        (The Countryside Agency)

Useful Organisations

Bath and North East Somerset Council
The Guildhall, High Street, Bath BA1 5AW
Tel. 01225 477000
www.bathnes.gov.uk

British Waterways
The Locks, Bath Road, Devizes, Wiltshire SN10 1QR
Tel. 01380 722859
www.britishwaterways.co.uk

Campaign to Protect Rural England
128 Southwark Street, London SE1 0SW
Tel. 0207981 2800
www.cpre.org.uk

Camping and Caravanning Club
Greenfields House, Westwood Way, Coventry CV4 8JH
Tel. 0845 130 7633
www.campingandcaravanningclub.co.uk

English Heritage
1 Waterhouse Square,138–142 Holborn, London EC1N 2ST
Tel. 020 7973 3000
www.english-heritage.org.uk
Regional office
Tel. 0117 975 0700

Mendip Hills AONB
Charterhouse Centre, Blagdon, Bristol BS40 7XR
Tel. 01761 462338
www.mendiphillsaonb.org.uk

Natural England
1 East Parade, Sheffield S1 2ET
Tel. 0845 600 3078
www.naturalengland.org.uk

The National Trust
Membership and general enquiries
PO Box 39, Warrington
WE5 7WD
Tel. 0844 800 1895
www.nationaltrust.org.uk
Wessex Regional Office:
Eastleigh Court,
Bishopstrow,
Warminster, Wiltshire
BA12 9HW
Tel. 01985 843600

North Somerset Council
Town Hall,
Weston-super-Mare
BS23 1UJ
Tel. 01934 888 888
www.n-somerset.gov.uk

Ordnance Survey
Romsey Road, Maybush,
Southampton SO16 4GU
Tel. 08456 05 05 05 (Lo-call)
www.ordnancesurvey.co.uk

Public Transport
Traveline
Tel. 0871 2002233
www.traveline.org.uk

Quantocks AONB
Fyne Court, Broomfield,
Bridgwater, Somerset
TA5 2EQ
Tel. 01823 451 884
www.quantockhills.com

Ramblers
2nd Floor, Camelford House,
87-90 Albert Embankment,
London SE1 7TW
Tel. 020 7339 8500
www.ramblers.org.uk

Somerset County Council
County Hall, Taunton TA1 4DY
Tel. 0845 345 9166
www.somerset.gov.uk

Somerset Wildlife Trust
Somerset Wildlife Trust,
Tonedale Mill, Tonedale,
Wellington TA21 0AW
Tel. 01823 652400
www.somersetwildlife.org

South Somerset District Council
Brympton Way, Yeovil,
Somerset BA20 2HT
Tel. 01935 462462
www.southsomerset.gov.uk

Tourist information
www.visitsouthwest.co.uk

*Local tourist information
centres*:
Axbridge: 01934 750 833
Bath: 0906 7112000
Bridgwater: 01278 436 438
Burnham-on-Sea:
01278 787852
Cheddar: 01934 744071
Clevedon: 01934 426 020

Frome: 01373 467 271
Glastonbury: 01458 832 954
Langport: 01935 462 462
Nether Stowey: 01278 733642
Sedgemoor Services:
01934 750833
Stoke Sub Hamdon:
01935 829 333
Street: 01458 447384
Taunton: 01823 336344
Watchet: 01984 632 101
Wells: 01749 672552
Weston-super-Mare:
01934 888 800
Yeovil: 01935 845 946

Youth Hostels Association
Trevelyan House, Dimple Road,
Matlock, Derbyshire DE4 3YH
Tel. 01629 592700
www.yha.org.uk

Ordnance Survey Maps
Explorer maps 128 (Taunton &
Blackdown Hills), 129 (Yeovil
& Sherborne), 140 (Quantock
Hills), 141 (Cheddar Gorge),
142 (Shepton Mallet &
Mendip Hills East), 153
(Weston-super-Mare), 154
(Bristol West & Portishead),
155 (Bristol & Bath) and 156
(Chippenham & Bradford-on-
Avon), Landranger maps 172
(Bristol & Bath), 173 (Swindon
& Devizes), 182 (Weston-
super-Mare), 183 (Yeovil &

Frome), 193 (Taunton & Lyme
Regis) and 194 (Dorchester &
Weymouth).

Answers to questions
Walk 1: The entrance could
only be reached by winding
between outlying defended
embankments, exposing an
enemy to attack from all sides.
Walk 2: An information panel
describes an accidental shot, let
off by a garrison soldier, which
hit the ammunition store and
caused an explosion.
Walk 3: A plaque tells that,
while taking shelter beneath it
during a storm, a Georgian
clergyman, the Reverend
Augustus Toplady, was inspired
to write the famous hymn, *Rock
of Ages*.
Walk 4: They are some of the
fantastic rock formations inside
Wookey Hole.
Walk 5: Carved on the ends of
the pews in the Church of St
Mary the Virgin.
Walk 6: Beech; many were
originally planted in the area as
hedges, but lack of maintenance
has let them grow to their full
height.
Walk 7: Three, and even the
bench behind was carved for
three bottoms, cheek by cheek
by cheek.

Walk 8: 1840.

Walk 9: A spring of crystal water issuing from a low, stone grotto, once the supply for the priory's brewhouse.

Walk 10: Eleven.

Walk 11: Three, with a hasp for a padlock and a modern lock as well. With more than one keyholder needed to open the chest, no person alone could tamper with its contents.

Walk 12: A brass plaque beside the lane on the right gives the date, October 1865 and the benefactor was the lord of the manor, James Green Esq.

Walk 13: Oak, but look closely at its leaves and acorns. The dominant species of the Quantocks is the sessile oak, whose acorns have no stalks but the leaves do. The common English oak has the opposite arrangement.

Walk 14: Simon Werman; you will find the letters of his name sculpted on one of them. His name also appears with the date 1560 in the church at Trull, south west of Taunton.

Walk 15: An eel. Eel fishing was an important industry for the small communities that inhabited the marshes.

Walk 16: At one step a week, it would take you all year to climb it.

Walk 17: Britannia.

Walk 18: Six, three pairs of two each side of the central passage.

Walk 19: St George; he is slaying the dragon.

Walk 20: Many pieces of slag still bear a high proportion of lead, and these weigh much heavier than ordinary limestone chips.

Pollarded willow trees in early morning sun